Introduct...

C000196668

Everyone loves to make animals and
scoubidous is great fun, rewarding and inexpensive. This book
aims to give you basic instructions to get you started but will
hopefully give you lots of ideas and inspriration for your own
designs.

There are projects to tempt all skill levels in this book. The 'we
like easy' section is a good place to start if you are new to
scoubidous but the zebra, unicorn and lizard are a little more
challenging!

All the stitches and techniques you will need are all explained
in the instruction section.

Please remember: scoubidous should not be given to very
young children, especially under 3's as there is an obvious risk
of strangulation and small components can easily cause
choking.

I hope you enjoy making the projects in this book and have
lots of fun whilst doing it!

Lets get started. . .

Scoubidou Frenzy is divided into 2 sections

The pink section is the instruction section.

The lavender section is the project section.

Contents

Instruction section

Project section

Getting Started . . .

Several projects in this book need nothing other than scoubi strands, wire, a few beads and eyes.

When you start to add pom poms, chenille, pipe cleaners etc. the range of projects is unlimited.

Start Knots 1 & 2

Knot 1

Take 4 strands. Tie them together at the top.
Open them up and spread them out as shown in the picture.

Knot 2

Take 2 strands and fold them in
half to find the centre. Tie a
knot leaving loops at the top, which
are large enough for you to attach
your accessories.

Variation

Make a loop with just one strand and tie the second strand as shown.

This is useful when working on
spiral or plait stitch. It is also
useful for some key rings, zip pulls
or scoubis for your bike.

To Start Using Knot 1

To start, using knot 1 and 2.
Using the purple strand, make a loop facing forwards.

With the blue strand, make a loop by taking the strand behind. You should now have 2 loops, one purple and one blue.

Thread the right hand white strand through the purple loop.

And then the pink strand through the blue loop. Pull all strands firmly but carefully using equal tension.

You should end up with a base that looks like the picture opposite.

You can now choose which stitch to use for your first project.

Start Knot 3

Take 2 strands and fold them in half to find the centre.

Holding strands between your thumb and index finger make one loop.

And then another below.

Next, thread the right hand strand through the top loop.

And then the left hand strand through the bottom loop.

Still holding the strands between your thumb and index finger, carefully pull strands to form your base knot.

Once you have the right shape in place, pull the strands firmly to form a secure base for your next stitches.

The Square Knot

The square knot is usually the first stitch to master. It is basically the same process as the starting knot – you just keep repeating the steps. You must make sure that you start with the base stitch. When you have completed a new stitch you should still have this shape. So...

Still holding the starting knot between your thumb and index finger, make a top loop, and then a bottom loop. Thread the right hand strand through the top loop and the left hand strand through the bottom loop. Carefully pull all stitches to form the knot. Go back and tighten stitches.

Note : on the second row the process is reversed, so the top loop is on the right and the left strand is threaded through. The bottom loop is on the left and the right hand strand is threaded through.

TIPS

- If you pull **extremely** tightly be careful not to snap the strands.

- If you make loose knots, your scoubi will grow faster but will have a different overall appearance.

- Quite tight looks neat and is probably the tension you are aiming for. It is the best way hide wire when reinforcing.

- Hand cream, butter, food etc. do not mix very well with scoubis. It makes them impossible to work because they become very slippery and will not stay in a knot.

If you are having difficulty understanding the instructions and illustrations, why not persuade an adult to learn and then show you how to do it!

The Triangular Scoubi

To start, use knot 1 and open out.

Stitch One
Make a loop with the white strand and place thread over the black strand.

Next, make another loop with the black strand and pass over the yellow strand. Thread the yellow strand through the first white loop.

Pull carefully until the stitch is neat and reasonably tight. You should have a triangular shape.

Stitch Two
Is worked in exactly the same way but starts with the yellow strand.

Stitch Three
Starts with the black strand.

The 4 Stranded Scoubi

This stitch has a similar end result to the more traditional round scoubi knot (but I find it a lot easier and faster). You can use any starting knot or as in the photograph, use a bead.

The photographs show the basic 4 stranded round scoubi stitch. If you use the same technique with 6 strands it then becomes a 6 stranded scoubi and so on. It is quite possible to work with 8, 10, 12 and more strands!!

Thread your strands through the bead and open them out.

Make a loop with the green strand and pass it over the white strand. Pass the white strand over the pink strand and the pink over the yellow. Thread the yellow strand through the green loop and carefully pull the strands to form the base.

Repeat these steps. You will find that you start with a different coloured strand each time.

The 8 Stranded Rectangular Scoubi

Find the centre of 3 threads. Hold them together and tie together with the 4th length. Open out as shown.

To start, using thumb and index finger to hold, make a vertical left loop with pink thread and a vertical right loop with pink thread. Sometimes it is easier to lay your strands on a flat surface when making the first stitch.

Start with the horizontal loops. Make a top black loop and a bottom black loop threading over and under the pink loops as you work.

Continue the same procedure for the remaining 2 lengths, therefore, making a top green loop and a bottom yellow loop, still working over and under the pink strands.

Carefully start to pull all the individual loops quite tightly together. Keep going back to individually tighten each strand into its final place.

If all has worked out correctly you should have a base showing 12 small squares. Think of the 4 squares on the base of the basic square knot! You are doing exactly the same but with 3 strands joined with one horizontal strand.

Repeat the steps until you reach the desired length.

The Spiral Knot

The spiral is easiest to start using knot 2.

This stitch will use the outside strands a lot faster than the supporting middle strands. Therefore, you will usually have to use strands double the length for the outside. The spiral stitch always starts using the right hand outside strand.

Stitch One

After tying a start knot, (page 4) lay your 4 strands flat with the knot on the back. Take the outside blue strand over the middle two strands but behind the outside blue left strand. You will have a sort of blue loop.

Next, take the outside left strand and thread behind the middle strands bringing it through the blue loop.

Pull carefully until the stitch is neat and reasonably tight.

Stitch Two

Arrange the strands facing upwards and repeat the stitch. As this stitch grows, the stitches will turn around the middle strands creating a spiral effect.

The Plait Knot

This knot has a similar construction to the spiral but ends flat. This makes it very comfortable for bracelets and necklaces. Like the spiral, this stitch will use the outside strands a lot faster than the supporting middle strands. The only difference starts with the second stitch.

Stitch One

Follow the instructions for the spiral stitch.

Stitch Two

This is the same technique but starting from the opposite side. So...

Take the outside left pink strand over the middle two strands but behind the pink strand on the opposite side. The right hand blue strand goes over that strand, behind the middle strands and comes through the loop on the left. Carefully Pull tight.

Stitch Three

Is the same as stitch one.

Stitch Four

Is the same as stitch two.

Completion

Tie a knot on the back of the work and pull tightly. Trim closely.

To end

There are several ways to complete or finish off your scoubi, this book shows you three different ways.

Method 1
The easiest of all, and quite reliable, is to pull the last stitch tightly and snip close to the ends.

Method 2
If you want to be really sure your last stitch will hold, use a drop of strong glue on the last stitch before cutting.

TIP
It is often better to pull the last stitch tight and leave overnight before snipping the ends. This encourages your scoubi to 'set' and generally prevents the last stitch unravelling.

Method 3
Take 2 diagonal strands and tie together tightly. Trim ends closely. Take the remaining 2 strands, again tie tightly and trim closely.

Reinforcing and Wiring

By reinforcing a strand or scoubi you can increase the flexibility and widen the range of projects you can make. It is much easier to shape your creation when it is wired.

Using knot 3

When using knot 3 you can use one of two methods.

The more secure method is to attach a length of wire, which has been folded in half, on the bottom strand whilst starting. Keep the wire central whilst making your stitches. Insert after the base stitch is completed and hold in place whilst working the first few stitches.

Remember to work around the wire as you knot keeping it hidden in the middle. Cut the ends closely and bend into the shape you require.

Increasing and Decreasing

To increase or decrease is easy. To increase, you just add as many extra strands as you need whilst working.

Make a stitch but do not pull too tightly, you simply thread the strand you want to add under the loose stitch and then pull the remaining strands tightly.

To decrease, you just continue working the row but leave the strands you want to decrease unused and trim them close to your work.

To Make a Hole

This is a very easy technique to use and is also useful when making animals. Making a hole whilst working allows you to thread strands easily and neatly into the place you need them.

All you need is a pencil or cocktail stick — the size of the hole will depend upon the size of the object you use!

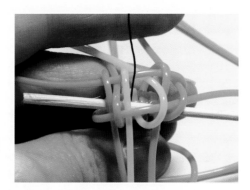

The technique is the same whilst working in any stitch.

When you reach the spot to make a hole, work a row, but before pulling the stitches tight slide your pencil or cocktail stick under the stitches.

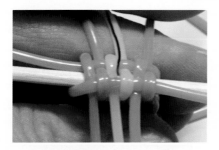

Now pull all the stitches tightly over the stick. I prefer to use a cocktail or bamboo stick because you can snap them into any length and leave them in place which makes them easier to work around until you are actually ready to use the hole.

To Make Ears

Lay your ears over the top of your work securing them with another stitch. Work the ears into position and pull the strands tightly to secure

Snazzy Snake

(Photo on page 32)

This is a snazzy snake with attitude. He is very easy to make but takes a little time

Tie an elastic band around the 4 strands and 41cm wire about 1cm from the end. Work in 4 stranded stitch for 17cm. Decrease 1 strand and work in triangular stitch for approx 8cm. Trim the wire to the end of your snake.

Thread the 3 strands through the bead and tie 2 diagonal knots to secure.

Use the template (page 32) to cut 1 x mouth and tongue. Remove the elastic band and cut both the wire and strands level with the top of the work. Fold the mouth in half, glue the tongue in the centre and then glue both the pom poms on top. Finish by adding eyes.

Curl your snake into position and admire!

Variation

The snake opposite is a more advanced version which uses the same method of construction with 12 strands. Work 27cm with 6 stranded round stitch. Decrease 2 stitches and work 4 strands for 8cm and then decrease 1 strand and work 3 strands for another 7cm. (Before you completely run out of a length of strand you need to introduce a new strand. Look at how to increase on page 13).

> ### You will Need:
>
> 4 x 100cm strands
> 1 x pony bead
> 2 x large eyes
> wire / glue
> 2 x pom poms 12mm
> felt/foam scraps
> elastic band

Octopus

My youngest daughter devised this project especially for the "we like it easy" section.

Take both strands and cut in half to make 4 x 50 cm lengths. You now need to use double strands throughout.

Slide two strands through the bead to the central point. Take the remaining 2 strands and tie a knot under the bead. Work 4 knots round, square or spiral all work well. Cut 8 x 30 cm lengths of wire and reinforce each strand as shown.

Fold the 8 strands over the knotted scoubi and secure with the pipe cleaner scrap. Open out the strands and position into place.

Glue on the eyes.

You will Need:

2 x 100cm strands
1 x pony bead
2 x 18mm eyes
wire / glue
pipe cleaner scrap

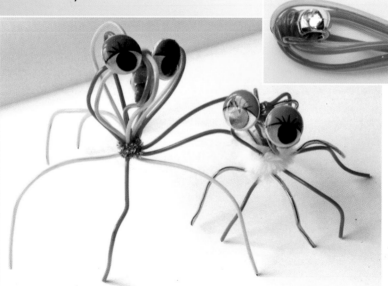

The lavender section

Butterfly

A very fast and easy project.

Use a looped knot and work a 4 cm length in spiral stitch. Tie a knot to secure the outside strands and trim the two outside strands closely.

Thread the two central strands through the bead and trim the ends to about 4 cm.

Cut 2 x 4 cm lengths of wire and push them into the two strands, try to push them down as far as possible. Bend the ends into shape.

Cut one set of wings using the template and glue onto the body. Then glue the magnet onto the back of the wings and finally glue on the eyes.

You will Need:

2 x 50 cm strands
1 small wooden bead
2 x eyes
funky foam / wire
Small magnet

Variation

The blue butterfly has a loop instead of a magnet. Make a loop with one of the outside strands and tie a tight knot and hide it under the head bead, if possible. You can then attach your butterfly to all sorts of things. – Why not make a mobile!

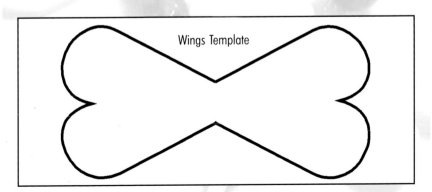

Wings Template

Mice

These appealing creatures look good in any colour. They are a little 'fiddly' at first so are not the best project for a beginner but they are definitely worth the effort.

You can adapt the basic instructions to suit yourself, the picture shows mice made using pipe cleaners and chenille for ears and tails as well as reinforced scoubi strands.

You will Need:

4 x 50cm strands
1 x 25cm strand
2 x eyes
wire
glue

If you are going to use reinforced strands for the ears and tail, reinforce 1 x 14 cm (tail) and 1 x 11 cm strand (ears).

Now take 3 strands and tie together at the central point with the 4th strand. Before pulling tight, slide the 14 cm reinforced strand through the knot. You need to leave at least 5 cm at one end. Now work an 8 stranded round scoubi (see page 9) over the 5cm that you left for approx 1 cm. (4 stitches) Put aside and then make the ears (if you are using chenille, you may find it easier to secure with a piece of wire or thread).

Lay your ears over the top of your work secure them with another stitch (see page 14). Make another stitch over the top. Work the ears into position and pull the strands tightly to secure. Work one more row. Decrease 2 strands on the next row and then work 1 more row using the 6 strands you have left. Decrease 2 more stitches on the next row (4 strands) and decrease 1 more strand on the final row (3 strands) Work one row of triangular stitch and then tie a diagonal completion knot (see

page 12) to shape the face. Trim the reinforced wire to 5 mm and bend over to make the nose.

Glue eyes and shape tail.

An easier way to make mice ...

Start by reinforcing your tail strand.
Fold the 50 cm strand in half and tie onto the tail strand leaving 3cm at one end. Make sure you have 25cm each side.

Substitute the tail strand for central strands
Work in plait stitch for $2^1/2$ cm. Pull the last 2 stitches tighter than the previous stitches to shape the face.

Fold the tail end strand over your work leaving a small nub for the nose. Turn your mouse upside down and continue making plait stitches over the ones you have already made until you have about 2 stitches left. Tie a knot on the underside of your mouse and trim the ends.

Glue the eyes on the right side of your mouse.

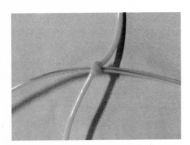

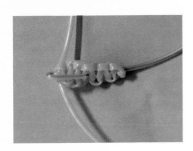

Rabbits

Once you have mastered the basic square stitch and the 8 stranded rectangular stitch these rabbits are plain sailing! The rabbit can be made into a brooch, magnet or keyring.

You will Need:

5 x 100cm strands
2 x eyes
glue

To start, take 2 strands and make a start knot 3. Work in square stitch for 2cm to form the first ear. Repeat this stage for the second ear.

Now you need to join the ears together. Place the ears side by side positioning them so as you can make 2 outside strands lie horizontally across the rest of your work. Work an 8 stranded rectangular stitch (see page 10) to fuse them together. Work in this stitch for another 2cm.

Take your last strand and cut into 4 equal 25cm lengths. Go back to the rabbit and work one more row, but, before pulling the stitches tightly thread a 25cm strand on each end. (these will be used to make the arms) You have to ignore these strands until you are ready to work with them.

Continue making the body for another 1½ cm. Then, divide the 8 body strands in half and start making the legs. Work each set of 4 strands in square stitch for 2½ cm.

Go back to the arm strands. Using the third 25cm strand and one of the embedded arm strands make a starting knot 3 and continue to work in square stitch for 2cm. Repeat using the last 25cm strand for the last arm.

Complete by gluing on the eyes.

Variation:

Why not make your rabbit into a necklace? Just attach a jump ring once the rabbit is finished to a long strand.

Variation: pom pom rabbit

Use the same principle as project 6. Work 2 x 4 stranded round scoubi for 1 cm (for ears)

Fuse using the 8 stranded rectangular stitch and work 2 more rows. then, decrease 2 stitches on the third row and another 2 stitches on the 4th row (shaping for the head)

Increase on the next row by using one of the strands you cut off, so as you can make the arms in triangular stitch. Thread the two remaining strands through the pom pom. Now tie on the remaining thread you cut off as close to the pom pom as you can. Using 3 strands work 3 cm in triangular stitch for leg. Repeat for the other leg. Finally finish with beads for hands and feet.

Glue on the eyes.

You will Need:

4 x 100cm strands
2 x eyes
1 x pom pom
glue

Variation: Rabbit Earrings

Exactly the same construction but reduced proportions! Make just 3 rows for the ears. Fuse together and work 2 more rows. Add a single strand for arms and then work a further 3 rows. Divide for legs and work 4-5 rows. Glue eyes and trim ends. Add earrings.

You will Need:

4 x strands
2 x scraps
4 x small eyes
2 x fish hooks

Tip:

Search through your strands and find the thinnest because not only are they lighter, they are also smaller when finished.

Crabs

You will Need:

4 x 100cm strand (green)
1 x 50cm strand (red)
2 x 7mm pom poms
2 x seed beads
wire / glue

The crab uses a completely different starting technique which is very easy.

From the red 50 cm strand cut: 3 x 8 cm pieces, 1 x 12 cm piece and 1 x 4cm piece. Reinforce all these pieces.

Take 1 green strand and find the central point. Individually tie the remaining 3 green strands onto the central point of the first strand.

Make the body by using 8 stranded rectangular stitch. Before pulling the first row of stitches tightly, thread the 4cm reinforced strand to make mandibles.

Work 2 more rows and insert the 12 cm strand. Work another 2 rows and insert an 8cm strand for legs. Work 1 more row add in a 8cm strand and repeat the last stage for the remaining set of legs.

Decrease 2 strands on the next row. work 1 row with 6 strands and pull tight and trim ends.

Bend pincers and legs into shape . Glue the pom poms into place and add the seed beads for the finishing touch.

Variation: Baby crab

The baby crab uses exactly the same technique but with reduced proportions.

Start by tying on just 2 strands and working a 6 stranded rectangular stitch.

Add a set of legs on each following row.

Finally decrease 2 strands on the last row (4 strands)

You will Need:
3 x 50cm strands (gold)
1 x 50cm strand (bronze)
2 x 7mm pom poms

Spider

Slightly adapt this technique and use black or dark coloured strands to make a spider. The pictures show 3 different ways to present your spider.

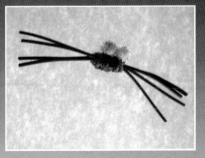

Unicorn

This mystical creature is not a project for a beginner.

Start to make a back leg by taking 4 strands and threading the ends through a pony bead leave about 5 mm of ends sticking out. Poke a piece of wire, approx 12 cm long into the middle of the strands and bead.

Work in round stitch for 3½ cm, making sure that the wire is the middle and is always surrounded by the strands - a reinforced round scoubi. Repeat this step with the other 4 strands. Put the two back legs side by side and join together using the 8 stranded round stitch. Work one more row and thread a piece of chenille approx 9 cm under the central stitch before pulling tightly to secure. Work one more row with 8 strands.

Increase on the next row to 10 strands. Continue working with the 10 strands for 2 cm. Cut your remaining strand into 2 x 50 cm. Work one more row but before pulling tight thread in the 2 new strands evenly – you need 25cm each side – pull tightly to ensure that the neck strands are embedded firmly. Work one more row with the original strands ignoring the newly introduced strands Isolate the neck strands with wire, or a paperclip until you need to work with them.

Divide the 8 strands in half, making sure that each leg still has one piece of wire ,and start working the front legs. Using 4 strands and round stitch, work until the front leg is the same length as the back leg. (approx 3 1/2 cm) Thread the four strands and wire through the pony bead and pull into place snugly. Repeat for the other front leg.

Back to the neck. Work 1 row using 4 stranded round stitch. Increase by 2 strands and work approx 2cm with the 6 strands. Make a pair of ears by using an 8 cm reinforced scoubi. Insert as shown on page 14. Work 1 more stitch with the 6 strands to secure. Decrease 2 strands on the next row. Choose the most suitably positioned strand to keep and use for a horn before decreasing by one more stitch on the next row.

Work 1 row using 3 strands and finish by using 3 diagonal ties to help shape the face. Thread a piece of wire into the horn strand and curl using a very thin cocktail stick. Glue 6 cm of chenille onto the neck for mane and a smaller amount around the horn. Finally, glue on the eyes and trim all strands to neaten.

Variation: Giraffe

There is only one real different aspect to the giraffe. You start using 2 white and 2 orange strands and a knot 3 instead of a bead for the legs. You can now continue with the same basic construction.

Substitute a reinforced scoubi strand for the tail and make the mane by threading scoubi scraps into one edge of the neck whilst working – no horn!

Zebra

Take 4 strands and cut into 8 x 50 cm lengths. Work in round stitch throughout the whole project.

To make a back leg, take 2 black and 2 white strands and thread the ends through a pony bead - leave about 5 mm of ends sticking out. Poke a piece of wire, approx 12 cm long into the middle of the strands and bead. Knot a 2cm length making sure that the wire is the middle and is always surrounded by the strands - a reinforced round scoubi. Repeat this step with the other 4 strands.

> ### You will Need:
> 3 x 100cm black strands
> 3 x 100cm white strands
> 4 x pony beads
> 2 x eyes
> wire / glue
> 12cm black chenille
> 6cm white chenille

Put the two back legs side by side and join together using the 8 stranded round stitch. Work one more row and thread a piece of chenille approx 6 cm under the central stitch before pulling tightly to secure.   Continue to make the body for another 2¹/₂ cm.

Cut your remaining 2 strands into 3 x 33 cm lengths. Work 1 more row but before pulling tight introduce 2 new strands (position evenly – you need approx 16cm each side) and pull tightly to ensure that the neck strands are embedded firmly. Work 2 more rows with the original strands ignoring the newly introduced strands

Divide the 8 strands in half, making sure that each leg still has 2 black, 2 white and one piece of wire, and start working the front legs. Work until the front leg is the same length as the back leg. (approx 2 cm)

Thread the four strands and wire through the pony bead and pull into place snugly. Repeat for the other front leg.

Back to the neck. Increase by 1 strand on the first row and another strand on the second row. (8 strands) Now work 5 rows with the 8 strands.

Change to the 8 stranded rectangular stitch for 2 rows. Shape face by decreasing 2 central strands on the next row. Pull the horizontal stitches as tight as possible. Work 1 more row with 6 strands and then decrease 2 more stitches on the next row. Trim the wire close to your work and finish by tying 2 x diagonal knots.

Take both remaining chenille lengths and twist together. Then glue onto the neck for mane. Finally, glue on the eyes and trim all strands to neaten.

Variation: Pony

Use square stitch and 8 stranded rectangular stitch in one solid colour to make horses and ponies. the tail is a made using a chenille scrap and reinforced scoubi.

Lizards

Take the green and yellow strands and a 20cm piece of wire and tie with an elastic band 10cm from the end.

Work in 8 stranded rectangular stitch for 2cm. Make a hole (see page 14) and continue for a further 3cm in rectangular stitch. Make another hole. Work another 1½ cm in rectangular stitch and then decrease 2 green stitches on the next line and a further 2 green stitches on the next line (4 strands).

Work in 4 stranded round scoubi stitch for 6cm and then decrease 1 yellow strand and work 2½ cm with just 3 strands. Finish by tying diagonal knots.

You will Need:

6 x 100cm green strands
2 x 100cm yellow strands
1 x 100cm red strand
wire
glue
2 x eyes

Remove the elastic band. Increase 2 strands by introducing the red strand in the centre. Work 6 rows (10 strands). On the next row decrease 2 outside strands. Work 2 rows with 8 strands on the final row, position the red strands to make the tongue. On the final row, work with just the yellow and green strands making sure that the red tongue is threaded into the middle of the row to make it look tidy!

Go back to the holes and make the legs. Using the cut offs from your strands, reinforce 2 x 8cm green and 2 x 8 yellow strands. Take one of each colour and twist. Thread through the hole and curl ends to make feet. Repeat for the second set of legs.

Glue eyes and trim ends.

Bugs
Creepy Crawlies

These bugs are amazingly life like and realistic, they are also very easy to make.

Work in square stitch for 1 cm. Add 1 of the 15cm reinforced strands for a leg.

You will Need:

2 x 50cm strands
4 x 15cm reinforced scoubidous
wire

Work 2 more square stitches and add another leg, then repeat for the 3rd leg. Now work just 1 square stitch before adding the last leg. Tie a diagonal knot leaving a small amount of each strand and trim to the length you want.

PROJECT 18

Another little beasty for you to make

Tie a looped knot and make 1 plait stitch. Add a leg by weaving your strand under the outside strands but over the central strands whilst making the next stitch. Work 7 more plait stitches adding a leg each time. Work two last plait stitches pulling them as tight as you can without snapping the strand.

You will Need:

2 x 50cm strands
8 x 5cm strands

Trim the two outside strands close to your work but leave the central strands approx 3 cm long

The lavender section

PROJECT 19

Grasshoppers

Make 2 stitches using a round knot. Reinforce
the 4 leg strands with wire and add 1 of the
9 cm strands whilst working your next stitch.
Repeat this step for the next 9 cm leg. Now
add the 5 cm leg with the next stitch and then
the final leg. Work 1 more stitch and pull
tightly. Thread all 4 strands through a bead.
Cut 2 pieces of wire 6 cm long and push them into 2 strands, try to push
them down as far as possible. Trim the 2 remaining strands close to the
edge of the bead and bend the 2 longer strands over and into shape.

Go back and shape the legs.

> **You will Need:**
>
> 2 x 50cm strands
> 2 x 5cm strands (legs)
> 2 x 9cm strands (legs)
> 1 small bead
> wire

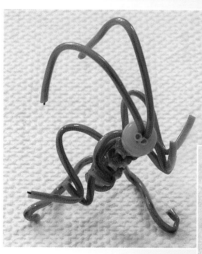

Variation:

There is no limit to the way you can make these creatures. Another
variation is to use a spiral stitch and just one set of legs. Instead of
leaving long strands you can curl them with a cocktail stick.

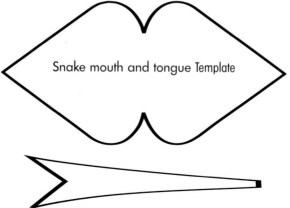

Snake mouth and tongue Template